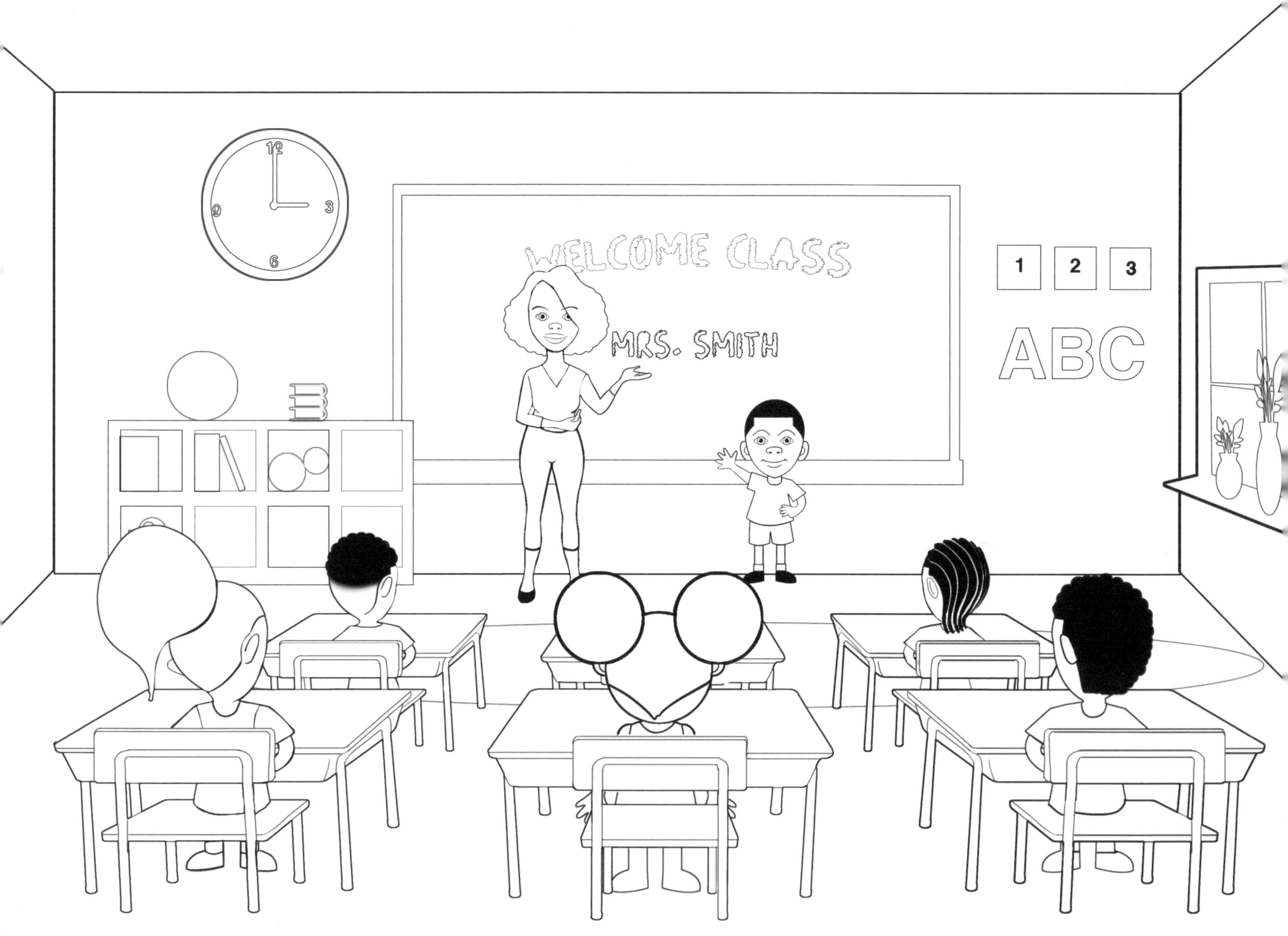
12
9
3
6
WELCOME CLASS
MRS. SMITH
1
2
3
ABC

12
9
3
6
WELCOME CLASS
RS. SMITH
1
2
AB

1
2
3
ABC

TALENT
SHOW

TALENT
SHOW

TALENT
SHOW

TALENT
SHOW

Printed in the USA
CPSIA information can be obtained
at www.ICGtesting.com
LVHW062149070124
768308LV00024B/11